Dear Me

Merlin Wei

Presentation by *BookLeaf Publishing*

Web: www.bookleafpub.com

E-mail: info@bookleafpub.com

ISBN: 9789357444750

First edition 2022

PREFACE

Hello, I am Merlin.

When I was writing these poems, "sharing" and "healing" were the keywords that came to my mind. These poems represent a period in my life that I still have emotional trouble with. Why not do something to record those feelings? I think that's why I started to write them.

Anyway, thank you for buying this book. This is the first book published in my life. I hope that you will enjoy reading it.

Artist

I don't want to be an artist.
The great artists live miserable lives:
sufferings and delights
all spring from their hands
onto the paper.
Desires and cries
all spring from their hearts
onto the paper.
And maybe,
maybe someone from far, far away will see.
I don't want to be an artist.
I want my life to be simple:
Three meals a day, one book a week, two movies
a month.
Not for anyone, not for anything
Not for yearning, not for praying.
Just for myself,
Live happily.

Birthday

On my twenty-fifth birthday,
I gave you back
your cufflinks, your bracelet, the money I owed
you,
and everything you left behind.
You took it,
and gave me back
my eyes of love, my words of joy,
my hands that write poetry, and my heart
glued with tape.
From now on, in this world,
two stubborn poets were born.

Possessive

Beloved, you said:
"Possessiveness is wrong
I never belonged to yours, and you
will never be mine."
Nonsense!
You possessed my smile, my tears,
simple pleasures,
and all my misfortunes.
Ah, and most of all,
you possess my time to crave and imagine.
If these are so-called "possessiveness"
then my existence is denied in its entirety.
You and I, standing face to face,
With a narrow, deep hollow
Between us.

Separation

The last conversation of last night
crossed my mind,
unexpected.
I forgot to share with you,
the fallen leaves of autumn here.
Alas, tell me please,
Why do separations have to happen?
Farewell, farewell,
Parting is the beauty of life.
If God exists
I pray to you sincerely.
Please grant mankind
the beauty of peaceful life,
the beauty of spirited heart,
the beauty of sweet love,
and the beauty of eternal loss.

Prison

White-winged planes
hover over the city.
Just like seagulls
hovering over the waves without wind.
Undulating constructions
roll like a flood without a voice.
In the surf, people delightedly sing.
Planes never want to prey on
those people,
so they turn around,
peck the crumbs by the sea on the ground.

Time

When my heart finds the one I care about the
most,
the sunset will never symbolize
the end of the day.
The shape of the moon will never
turn the leaves gray.
My love
in the sea of faces,
in this vast land,
in this endless universe,
Living lightly and cheerfully.

Cellphone

Switch on my cell phone, unconsciously,
and realized, I deleted the one I talked to the
most.
Putting down the phone as if I am abandoning it,
and become a free person:
missing no one, relying on no one.
It is easy to call someone,
And it is not hard to lose one.
My connections with others rely on my phone,
and I just want to throw it away.

Good Morning

Good morning.
Open my eyes,
try to make a sound,
as the world has never changed.
Nothing has been lost,
and nothing is forgotten.
Life tastes bitter after all,
like the rotten tea,
I have to find the sweetness in there
Again, again, and again.

Monsoon

From that day onwards,
It has been raining on Earth for two billion
years.
Who's been crying there,
For two billion years?
In this massive, solitary soul,
turning tears into the rain,
turning rage into the plain.
In this massive, solitary rain,
healing all the wounds and pain,
Burning all the hopes to drain.
And till that day
will be the end of the rain.

Fake Hope

I want to make a wish
In front of the falling leaves.
To hold your hand again
walk through countless days.
To appreciate
all the mountains on the way.
In the rustling north wind,
We are just passengers from another country.
To take your hand again
finding our home everywhere.

Decision

I woke up while the moon was drunk.
Another sunrise with no one to share with.
As usual, the clouds danced like fire on the edge
of the sky.
I watched with a peaceful mind.
I was still angry from the quarrel days ago,
but it's getting clear now:
without love
there is no room to tolerate what he has done.

The Stone of Dream

Dreams, as heavy as stones, squeeze my chest.
Why does the memory of you always shine with
despair?
I walk, step by step,
and step by step, nightmare bends my back,
shattered in the end.
I hate to remember them so clearly,
even the happiest squirrel could not drag them
away.
Standing in the street, I split into two
cold skin and a screaming heart.
If I run like the end of the world,
Will I find peace and rescue myself?

The Stone of Dream: Impossible

An impossible dream occurred.
It seems like that in order to give "it" to it,
The three of us went through the corridor of
memory.
"look, this is the café we've been to,
this is the path we walked."
I was mad,
To show off, to plead
It had a somewhat empty, somewhat cheerful
expression
I am sure I was the same.
Finally, we stopped and said,
"It is so nice to meet you."

Avocado

I thought I was calm.
But this morning, when I
opened up a fresh avocado from the past,
sliced, cored, and cut into two pieces
the smell of Down the Road dragged me
to the depths of my memory.
Soft, delicious avocado,
a joy of me ordering secretly.
Another thing that I love, but you don't.

Petrified

I walk on the street,
listening to the sound of tiny snow
touched by the wind.
The dry leaves are the tears of the trees.
Gathered under the roots,
like arms that never want to leave.
Like me waved to you
But you could never see.

Mermaid

I woke up from a long dream
like a mermaid,
floating above the sea for the first time
To breathe and watch.
There is a vague future,
Calling my name gently
By the shore over the sea.

Dear me

I walk to the future, with all the pain.
Four seasons slipped through my fingers,
with a deer behind, that I dare not to see.
She will sleep soundly and go with the wind.
The new journey starts already.
Under the wind and rain,
I shall keep walking.

Lover

We took the shells away from the body.
Eyes burning like polished amber,
with the shape of a water drop,
blazing thoroughly.
The night with spring breeze
crushing all the moonlight in the streets.
Speechless, for the pleasure of the body.
A soft pain comes from my stomach.
That's the gentle defense of the cold wind,
for the secrets buried deep